GOOD
TIMES
WITH
MAPS

By Irene Estep

Illustrated by

Robert Smith

MELMONT
LOOK ★ READ ★ LEARN

Melmont Publishers, Inc.
Chicago, Illinois

Also by Irene Estep   IROQUOIS

Library of Congress Catalog Card Number 62-7016

TABLE OF CONTENTS

pages

FOREWORD

A map is usually a drawing of some part of the earth as it might appear if one were up very high looking down on it.

When you first look at a map it may seem like a puzzle. It may seem to be made up of lines and marks and colors that have very little meaning.

Learning to use a map can be as much fun as working a puzzle or playing a game. There is a reason for each line and mark and color. Each is a help or a key in working the puzzle or playing the game.

This book will show you how to use one kind of map—the highway or road map. After you have learned to use it, you should be able to use almost any other kind. You should be able to have a good time with maps.

Most people travel about town in their automobiles. They also use cars to go from city to city and from one state to another.

Maps that show roads and highways are a great help to the traveler by car. There are highway maps for each state and for the different sections of the country. There are city maps; there are county maps.

In this book we are going to talk about a highway map of the whole United States and one of the state in which you live.

Perhaps there are copies of these two maps in the glove compartment of the family car. If not, Mother or Father should be able to get them for you. Automobile clubs and service stations often give these maps away.

Unfold both maps. Spread them out on the floor or on a big table.

Are you ready? All right! Then let's begin.

BOUNDARIES AND BOUNDARY LINES

Let's look first at your map of the United States. Look at the very top of the map. Is it a different color than most of the rest of the map? Do you find the word C A N A D A printed there in large letters? Many maps of the United States do show a part of the big country, Canada, that lies just to the north of the United States.

Now look at the bottom of the page. There you should find part of another country, M E X I C O. It, too, will probably be a different color.

There is a boundary line between your yard and the yard next door. Perhaps there is a fence between the two yards. If there is, you can see the boundary line. If there is no fence, you cannot see the boundary line but it is there just the same.

You might travel into Canada or Mexico from the United States without seeing a boundary line. But when men set up posts, build a fence, or put up a sign, you know the boundary line is there.

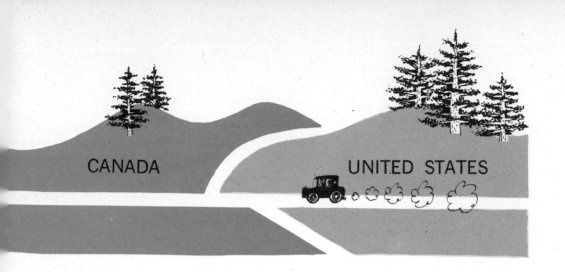

CANADA

UNITED STATES

On a map, boundary lines are plainly marked. They can be seen.

Look at your map of the United States again. Can you find the boundary lines between the United States and Canada? Between Mexico and the United States?

Boundaries are not shown the same way on all maps. The boundary lines on your United States map may be black or colored lines. They may be a row of dots · · · · · · · · · · · · · · · · · · Dots and lines may be put together in different ways ·—·—·—·—·—·—·—·—·—· ···—·····—····—··· Or boundaries may be shown by broken lines of different kinds — ·········

Sometimes a different colored line is used on each side of a boundary line to make the boundary easier to see.

All lines of this kind are the keys for finding the various boundaries on maps.

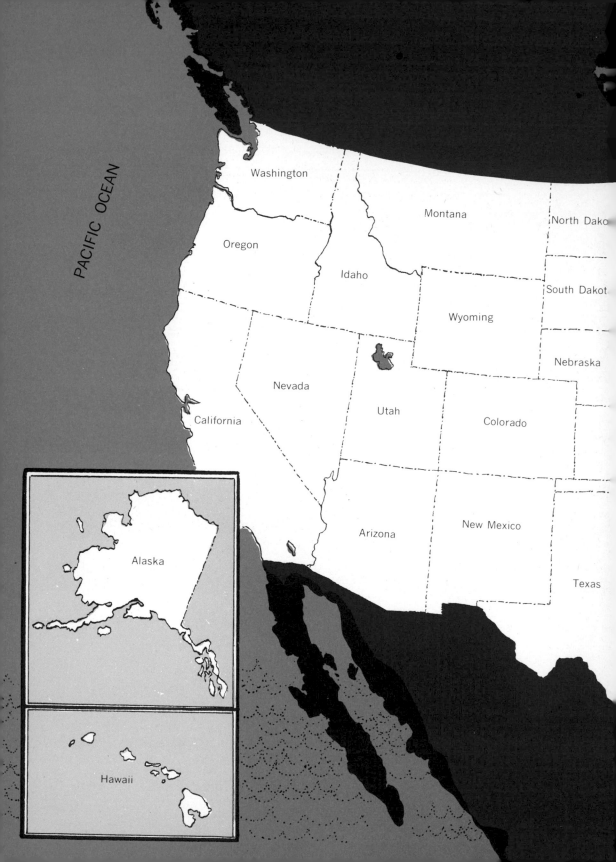

Minnesota

Wisconsin

Lake Superior

Lake Michigan

Lake Huron

Michigan

Lake Ontario

Lake Erie

St. Lawrence River

Maine

Vermont

New Hampshire

Massachusetts

Rhode Island

Connecticut

New York

Pennsylvania

New Jersey

Iowa

Illinois

Indiana

Ohio

Maryland

Delaware

West Virginia

Virginia

Kansas

Missouri

Kentucky

North Carolina

Tennessee

Oklahoma

Arkansas

South Carolina

Alabama

Mississippi

Georgia

ATLANTIC OCEAN

Louisiana

Florida

GULF OF MEXICO

9

There will be lines on your United States map to mark the boundaries between the states. Can you count forty-eight states? Alaska and Hawaii, our forty-ninth and fiftieth states, are far from the main part of the United States. You will probably not find them on your highway map.

Where do you find the names of states on your map? They may be printed across the middle of each state. Perhaps they are printed along the boundary lines.

The name of each state may be spelled out or it may have been shortened. When a word is shortened we say it is abbreviated. To abbreviate means to shorten. So, on the map you may find Wisconsin or Wis., New York or N.Y., South Dakota or S.D., and so on.

You found the boundary lines between the United States and Canada and Mexico. Now see if you can find the boundary lines on your state map that separate your state from the states that lie next to it. What are the names of the bordering states? Have you ever traveled into one of them? If so, could you tell when you crossed the boundary line?

Each state, except Louisiana and Alaska, is divided into smaller parts called counties. Louisiana is divided into parishes; Alaska into districts. Look for the county boundary lines on your state map. Look for the names of the counties. Do you know the name of the county in which you live? Can you find it on your state map?

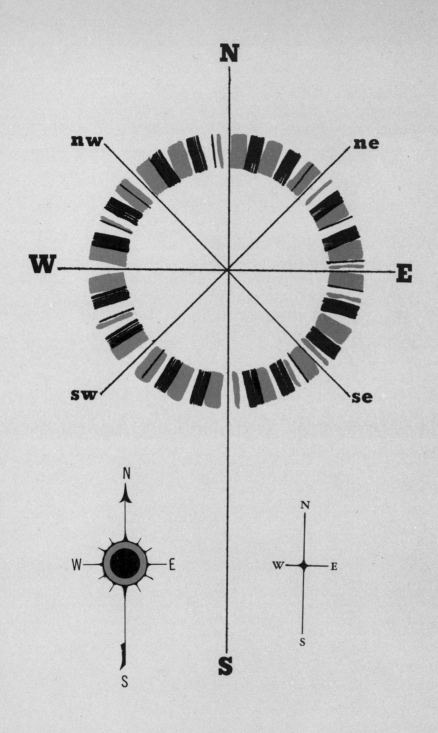

THE DIRECTIONAL SIGN

THE DIRECTIONAL SIGN

There is usually a key to finding directions on every map. The key may be an arrow pointing north, or all four directions may be shown in a circle. On some maps the directions are printed along the edges. Sometimes the directions are spelled out—north, south, east, and west. However, they are more likely to be shown simply as N.—S.—E.—W.

Can you find the directional sign on each of your two maps? North will probably be at the top of the map and south at the bottom. East will then be to the right and west to the left.

It is a good idea to face north when looking at a map. Then, if north is at the top of the map, and the map is right side up, its directions will be the same as your own.

THE MAP LEGEND

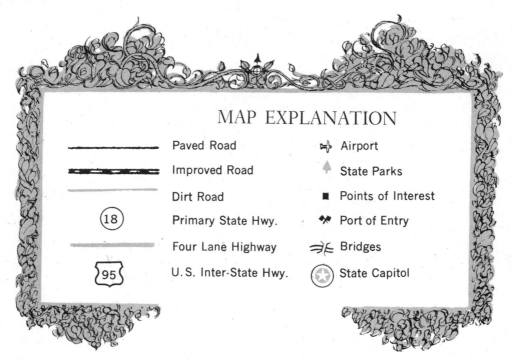

MAP EXPLANATION

————————	Paved Road	✈	Airport
▬▬▬▬▬▬	Improved Road	▲	State Parks
————————	Dirt Road	■	Points of Interest
(18)	Primary State Hwy.	⚒	Port of Entry
————————	Four Lane Highway	⊅⊱	Bridges
{95}	U.S. Inter-State Hwy.	⊛	State Capitol

    In one corner of each of your maps there should be a list of some of the more important keys used on the map. This list is usually called the LEGEND, though it may be called MAP EXPLANATION or something else. It may not be given any name on the map.

    The legend is there to explain some of the lines, marks, and even colors used on the map. Every map has its own keys. Don't make the mistake of thinking the keys for one map will fit some other map.

    As you use maps more and more, you will find that you look first at the legend to help you understand each map more easily.

THE SCALE OF MILES

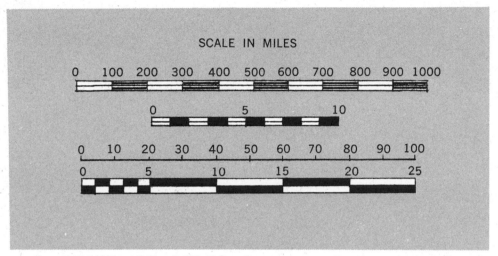

A SCALE OF MILES is part of the legend on every highway map. It is a line with marks on it much like those on a ruler. However, the marks show miles not inches. They are the key to measuring distance on the map.

The SCALE OF MILES on your two maps will not be the same because your state is only a small part of the map of the whole United States. One inch on the map of the United States may be equal to 128 miles. On the state map an inch may equal no more than 20 miles.

Using the SCALE OF MILES measure the length or the width of your state on each of the maps. Do you find that the number of miles is about the same in each case? It should be.

CITIES, TOWNS, AND VILLAGES

Large cities, and some not so large, will be shown on your United States highway map. Are the names of some of the cities printed in larger type than others? If so, do you know why? You guessed it! Names of large cities are printed in large type. Names of smaller cities are in smaller type.

In each state there is a capital city where the government of that state is carried on. Maps have different ways of showing the capital of a state. Perhaps your state map uses a star or a large colored dot.

See if you can find the capital of each of the states on your United States map. How can you be sure it is the capital?

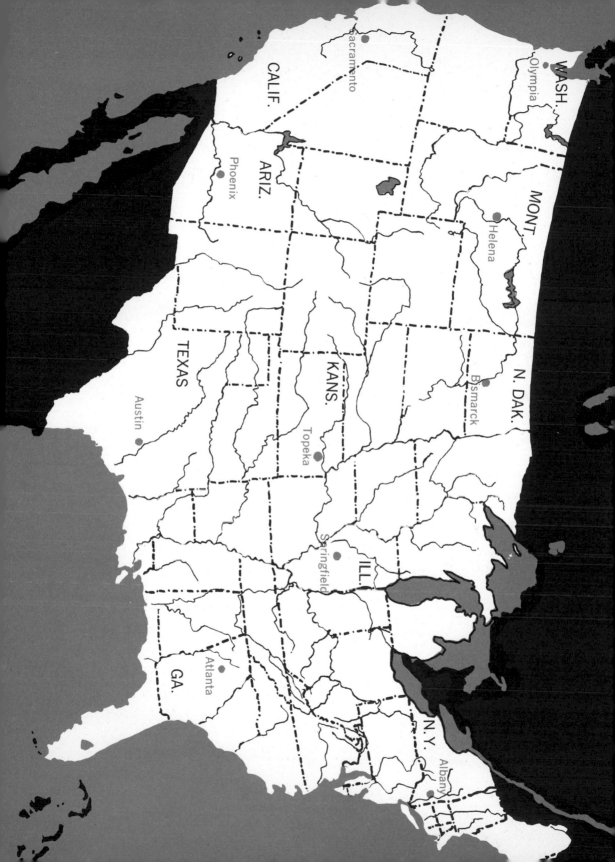

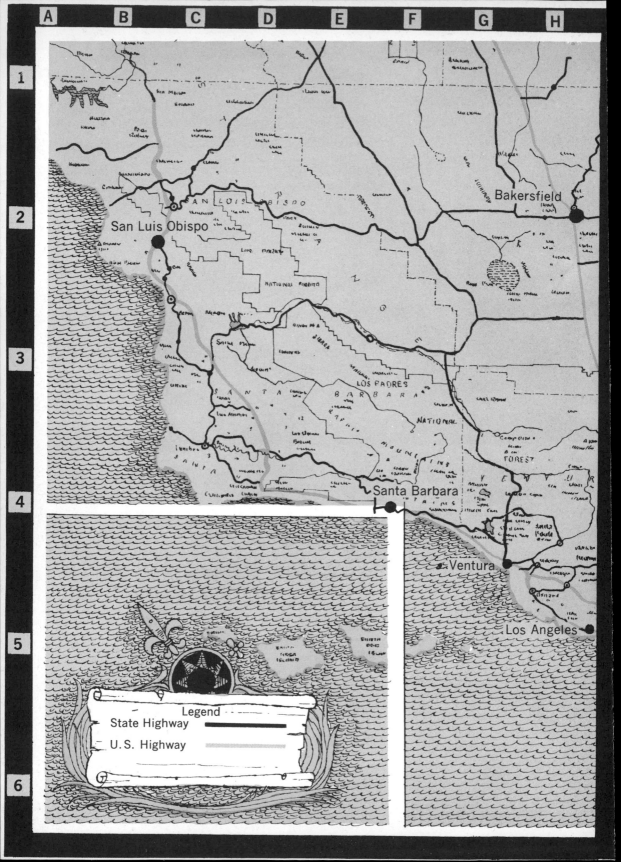

More of the cities and towns in your state can be shown on your state map than on the map of the whole United States. Because there is so much more space on the state map, even small villages can be shown.

So many places are marked on the state map that there has to be a key to help find them. A list of them is printed on the back or along the sides of the map. Do you find it? Is there a letter and a number after each name—like F 4, H 7, or B 10?

Look at the edges of the map. You should find letters printed along two edges, numbers along the other two. Let's learn to use these keys. Pick any town from the list. Suppose its symbols are F 4. Look for the letter F along one edge of the map and lay a strip of paper on the map from the letter. Now find the number 4 along another edge and do the same thing. The town should be near the place where the two strips of paper cross.

On the back or in one corner of your state map, you may find one or more small maps of some of the large, important cities in your state.

Even as small a map as this is a help to the visitor in a strange city. It shows him where the post office or a hospital may be found. It points out interesting places to visit such as a park, the museum, the zoo.

If there is a map of a city on your state map, study it. Find some places on it that you might like to go and see.

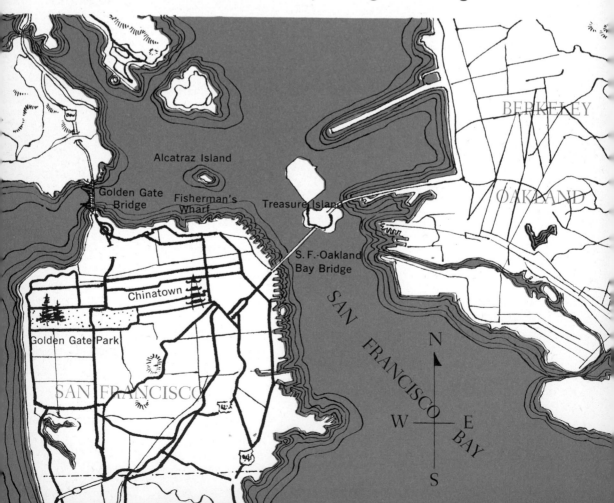

ROADS AND HIGHWAYS

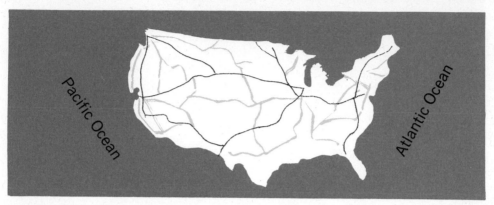

Roads and highways are always clearly marked on highway maps. On other kinds of maps they will not be shown at all.

Color will probably be one of the keys to roads on your United States map. A heavy red line is often used for those highways that run all the way across the United States or those that go from Canada in the north to Mexico in the south. Is this true of your map?

Blue or black lines may mark the shorter roads. There may be lines to show whether a road is paved or whether it is only a dirt or gravel road. Some highway maps show roads that are being worked on or where new roads are planned. This is a great help to the driver of a truck or car.

Does the legend on either of your two maps give keys that will help you find different kinds of roads on the maps?

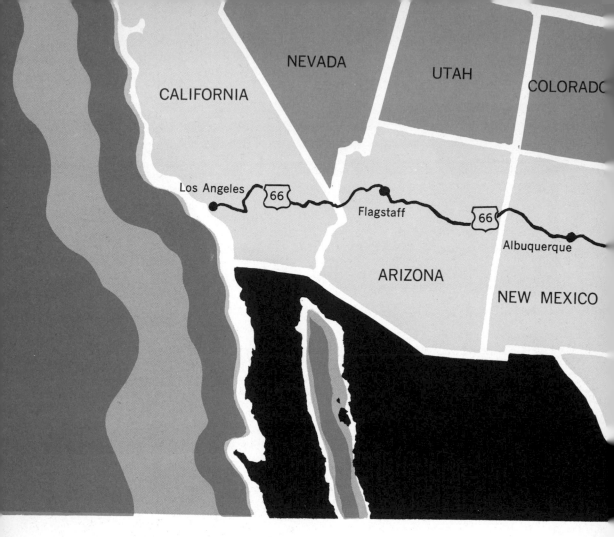

If you travel about much in an automobile, you know that almost every road has a number. Markers along the way show these numbers. The same numbers are used as keys to the highways on road maps.

Another special key on a road map is the shape of the line around each highway number. The numbers are usually inside a shield if the road is owned by the United States government. They are inside a circle or an oval if the road is owned by the state.

Find Los Angeles in California and Chicago in Illinois on your United States map. Do you see the number 66 near either of these cities? Try to trace highway 66 between Los Angeles and Chicago. Which states does the road pass through?

Highway 1 starts way down at the tip of the state of Florida and goes north up into Canada. Can you follow it on the map?

Highways owned by the United States will be shown on your state map if they run through your state. All of the state-owned roads should be shown.

Find a state-owned road on your state map that goes through the city or town in which you live. Does it cross the boundary line and go into the state that lies next to yours? When a state-owned road crosses a state line, the number of the road may change.

The shorter roads may be marked in other ways. The numbers may be printed in a different color or they may be inside a square. In some states a letter instead of a number is used to mark the less important roads.

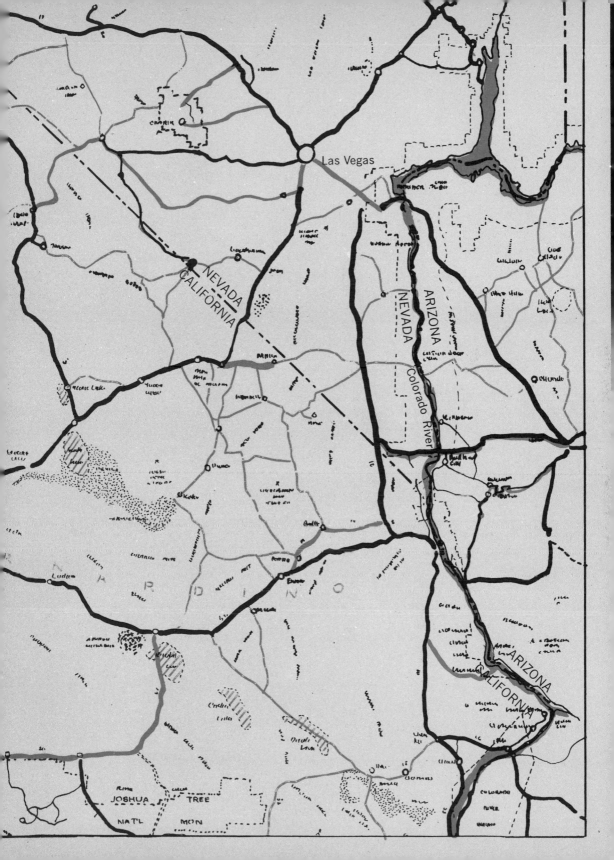

OCEANS, LAKES, AND RIVERS

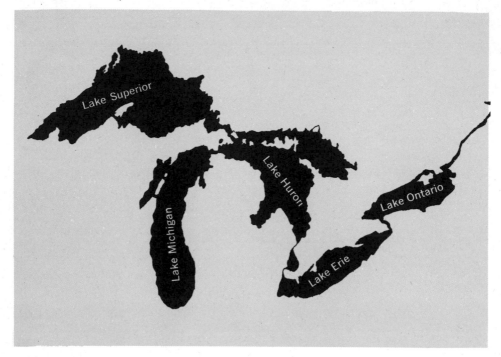

By this time you have probably discovered the large and small patches of blue on both of your maps. If you decided that blue is used to show bodies of water such as oceans, lakes, and rivers, you were right.

Looking at your United States map, find the Pacific Ocean on the western boundary. Then look for the Atlantic Ocean on the eastern boundary. What are the names of the lakes that form part of the boundary line between the United States and Canada? These five lakes together are known as the Great Lakes.

Can you find the Gulf of Saint Lawrence on the eastern boundary of Canada? What is the name of the river that flows from Lake Ontario into the Gulf of Saint Lawrence?

The Gulf of Mexico lies along the southern boundary of the United States. Do you see it on your map?

Look for some lakes and rivers on your state map. Perhaps the Mississippi River is one of the boundaries of your state. This big river flows all the way from Minnesota down to the Gulf of Mexico. It forms the boundary line between many states.

Have you ever looked down on a river from an airplane? If so you could see that the line the river makes on the land from way up there is much like the line it makes on a map.

If you live in Utah you know that the Great Salt Lake is in your state. Have you found it on your map? It is large enough to be shown on the map of the United States, too.

MOUNTAINS

Mississippi River

APPALACHIAN MOUNTAINS

Mountains are usually shown on a map by groups of tiny curved lines. Can you find any lines of this kind on your United States map?

There are mountains in some of the Eastern states, all of the Western states, but in very few of the Central states. The Ozark Mountains are in the state of Missouri. Do you also find them in Oklahoma and Arkansas?

What other mountains can you find marked on your two maps?

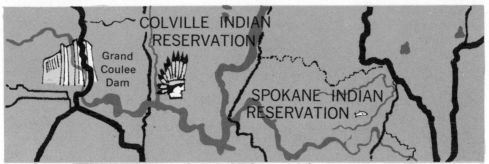

So many other interesting things are shown on your maps. You might like to play a game with yourself to see how many different things you can discover.

Here are just a few of the places to look for. Try to find a STATE PARK, a NATIONAL PARK, a NATIONAL FOREST. Perhaps you have visited one or more spots of this kind. If so you know how beautiful they can be.

Is there a BIRD REFUGE marked on your state map? This is a place where wild birds are kept from harm. It may be called a BIRD SANCTUARY on your map.

All over the United States land has been set aside as a home for the Indians. This land is called an INDIAN RESERVATION. Is there a reservation in your state? Can you find several reservations on the United States map?

The game is not ended. You are now on your own. Have a good time with your maps.

OTHER MAPS

There are many different kinds of maps. Geographical maps, the kind found in geography books, are perhaps the most common. You will use more and more of them as you study geography and history. They are much like highway maps except that they do not show roads and highways.

Maps are sometimes bound together into a book to make what is called an atlas. They may be an atlas of the United States, of Europe, of Asia, of any continent. In a World Atlas there is a map for every country in the world.

A globe is a map of the whole world. It is round like the earth. It is made to turn around its center because our earth moves this way.

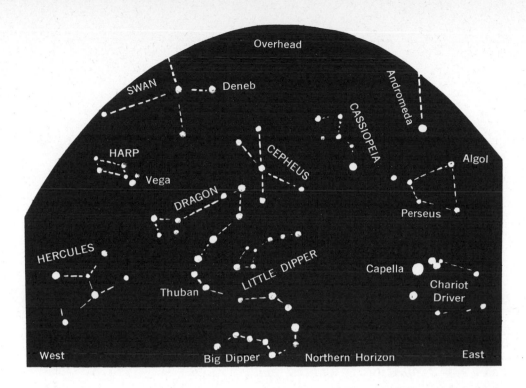

Maps can be made to show a great many different things. A map may point out where various crops are raised. One map may trace the routes taken by birds when they fly south each autumn. Another map will show the travels of the early explorers. There are weather maps. There are sky maps that show the position of the stars at different seasons of the year.

You will find maps in newspapers, in magazines, in books. Remember to look for the legend on each map. It will give you the keys that will make the map easier to understand and to use.

Irene Estep grew up on the central plains but has since lived in various parts of California. It was as a member of the Ventura County Writers' Club that Mrs. Estep really began to take writing seriously. She was rewarded by having a number of poems published.

In the years that followed, she furnished eight newspapers in the Los Angeles area with material. She also wrote an occasional column for a local paper. It was not until she began to write for children, however, that Irene Estep found the joy and satisfaction she was looking for in her work. She says: "Having no children of my own, I have adopted a large family of young readers who write to tell me that they like my books." She has to her credit five books in a Pioneer Series published by Benefic Press in addition to one other Melmont book.

Mrs. Estep and her husband make their home in Sunnyvale, California.

Robert Smith received his art training at the Art Center School and the California School of Art, both located in Los Angeles. He is carving out a career for himself as a commercial artist. Some of his illustrations have appeared in Westways Magazine.